Brand van Egmond
Lighting Sculptures

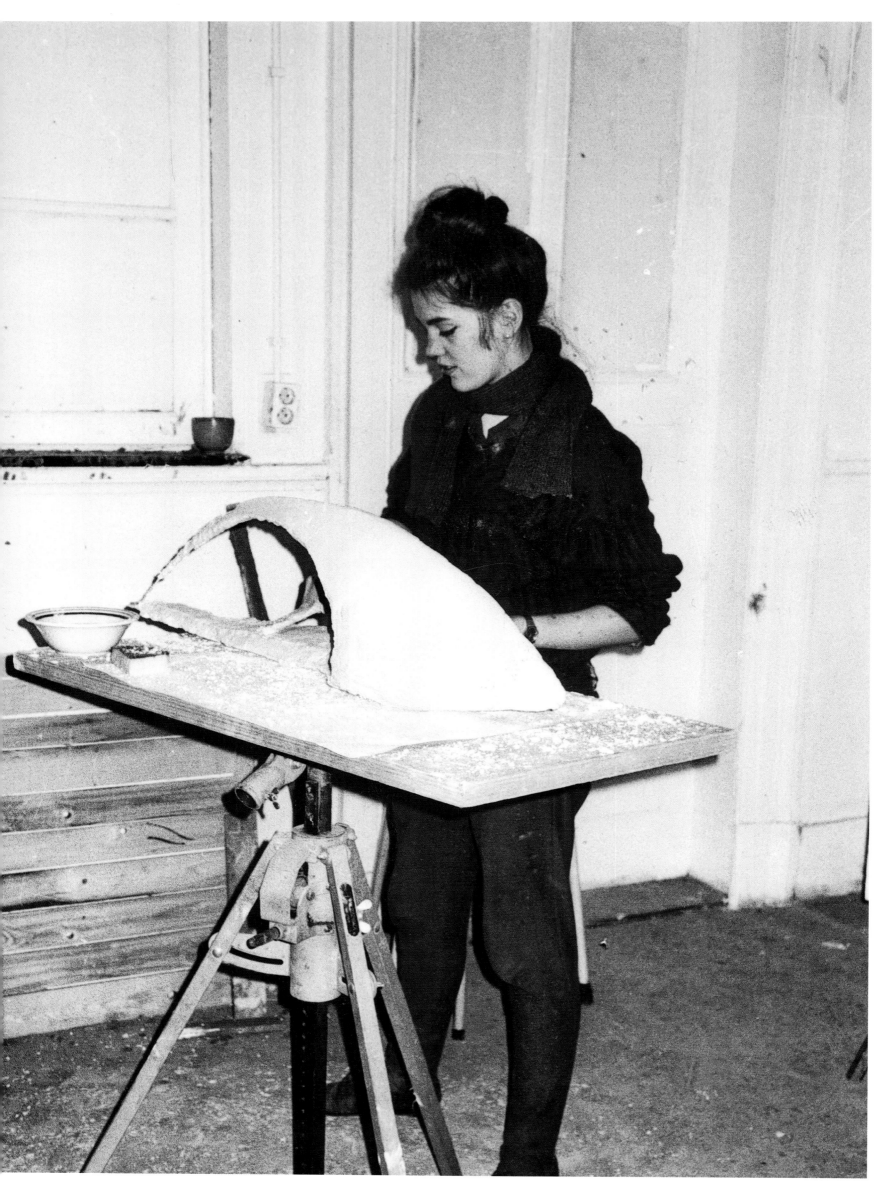

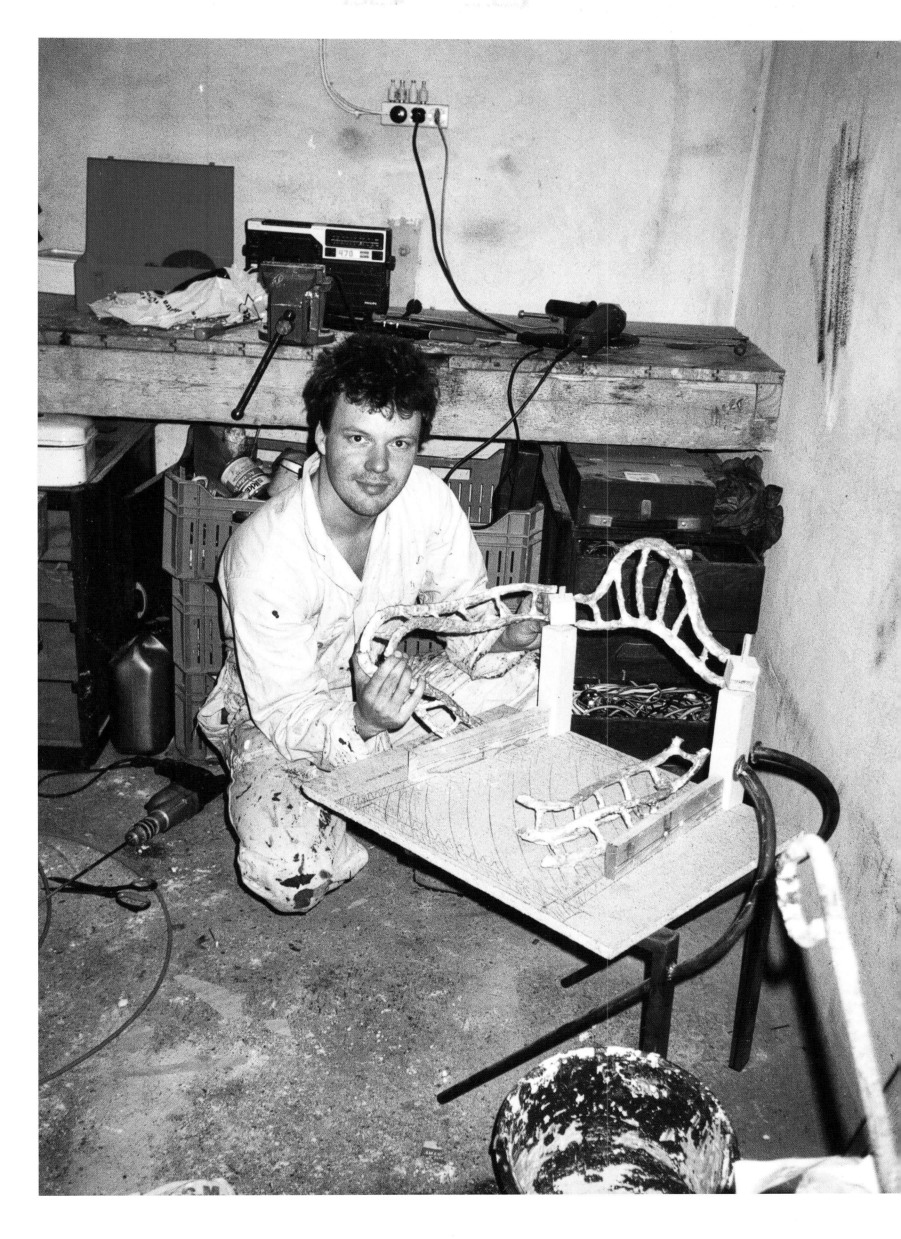

Brand van Egmond

Lighting Sculptures

TERRA

Foreword

Some words are simply not used for interior or design products. *Sexy* for example. But how can one otherwise describe a mysterious black chandelier that is held together by rings and laces, like a corset, which evokes notions of the female nude, of boudoirs, of perfume by Caron? Or *fashion*? And what can you say when Swarovski crystals form the flush of glamour that transforms iron into a jewel that illuminates a room? *Romanticism*? – the appropriate word for the modern chandeliers that light up softly between flowers and leaves of steel. Or *poetry* – the sweet memories of grandma's party cakes elaborated into a friendly light-radiating object, or the suspended lamps with crystal icicles as if they were made for an Ice Queen. Or what about *passion*? After all, what else does the rose with the light between its leaves wish to communicate, a flower of steel, alone or combined to form a bouquet, like a gift from an ardent lover?

These are lamps, but also primarily works of art that touch the emotions and the heart, these shimmering objects by Annet van Egmond and William Brand, she a sculptor, he an architect, both artists. I know nothing about their relationship, but from the moment they met one another at the Hogeschool voor de Kunsten in Utrecht (Utrecht School of the Arts), they seemed so united, so evidently accomplices, that I easily suspect a bond of love and much more.

There is a lightness and happiness in the souls of these exceptional designers. They are not seeking an industrial product as such, but rather a unique item, made to measure for a client or principal, as the crystallisation of a personal longing. They astonish, charm, surprise, confuse, seduce and move. They create atmospheres, convert a room into a theatre, a ceiling into a place where dreams arise.

We were used to lamps with geometrical forms, austere lines, rational variants, based on technological research, fascinating in their measured and decorative style reduced to the essence. The lamps created by Brand van Egmond totally invert this concept and allow free access to fantasy and influence. They carry the eclectic design movement of the third millennium to the extreme with the addition of sensuality and magic. After standardised *industrial design*, they give us a personalised *artistic design*.

Gisella Borioli
Journalist and art director

Dutch Autonomy

'Twenty Years'

—

We are often asked where our passion for light and sculpture comes from, how it developed and how we reached our present position. To be honest, we ask ourselves the last question every day too. Perhaps it was through our love of the craft, our enthusiasm and the desire to discover new things, a bit like an archaeologist who is excavating and not knowing what he will find. When it comes to answering the first question, the birth of our passion for lighting sculptures, our time at art college was very important. I sometimes compare that period to 'the Big Bang', the original explosion that created the universe. It was possible to experiment at college. We learnt to weld for the first time and we made our prototypes and sculptures separately; we photographed and did sketches and drawings. We saw something magical in these unfamiliar things. It was an exciting, chaotic brew of discoveries, and at the time we did not know where they would lead. That only became clear later.

1989 saw the birth of our first lighting sculpture, *Chandelier*. It was born out of masses of sketches of gourds. For the first time we raised a sculpture from the floor to the ceiling. And so, unintentionally, we created our first lighting sculpture. We initially thought this was a one-off project, but we gradually realised that light and sculpture could be interwoven to create a whole new experience.

Our first commissions made us very happy. We learnt a lot from the designers and clients we worked with, but we remained freelance. Despite the unremitting labour, the many long days and welding fumes, this was the approach that made us happiest. In that period we did not want our concentration to be broken so we worked on our own. At first we peddled our collection to manufacturers, but they simply were not interested. We did not want to lose any time so for the first eight years we made everything ourselves, just the two of us. In the end we realised that our independence gave us the unique opportunity to continue creating autonomously.

I think our passion stems from the endeavour to make each year's collection better than the last, and of even more enduring quality. The urge to develop and to grow is a significant driving force. You have to keep on improving on yourself. We are now celebrating our twentieth anniversary, but we still experience every day as the start of a new journey. We would like to show you the ground we have covered with our lighting sculptures over the last two decades, using a wide range of photos, many of which are from our personal albums.

Annet van Egmond

Welcome to the Garden of Amsterdam

'The House is a Home'

—

In the Gooi area, commonly called 'the Garden of Amsterdam', there is a monumental villa built in 1898 that displays the characteristic Brand van Egmond touch. It is the home of William Brand and Annet van Egmond and their two sons. They bought the house in 1996, prior to which it had for forty years been the 'Music School of Gooi and the Vecht Region'. Something which at first looked like an impossibly and much too risky project (when they first went to view the house William was already thinking of turning back before they got up the drive) turned into a house that has never since loosened its hold on them. In addition to its excellent location, the villa turned out to have a typically Dutch classical austerity and the rooms were ideally and harmoniously arranged. The decision was taken, more with the heart than the mind. But a great deal still had to be done before it became the perfect private setting for their lighting sculptures.

The house was packed with countless home-made soundproofed rooms where music lessons were given and dozens of skips full of waste were removed before the building was reduced to its bare essentials. The arrangement of the house was good and felt right, so nothing needed to be done on that score. The rooms were not too big and not too small. They decided to start living there while building work was still going on, so as to closely supervise progress. William took on the role of architect and did the drawings for the conversion himself. The principle behind the restoration was to respect the period when the house was built and to cherish the soul of the building. However, at the same time it also had to be adapted to modern standards. William designed cupboards and details to create the impression that they had stood the test of time. All the annoying electrical cables and pipes were concealed in the walls and account was taken of the need to install monumental lighting sculptures that would have to hang from the plain ornamental ceilings. The fact that, while building work was going on (which in the end took two years) they lived for at least six months in the uninsulated attic with their two-year-old son and just an electric heater, microwave oven and a couple of thick blankets, fits in entirely with the optimistic pioneering mentality with which William and Annet tackle every project, and it is also characteristic of the way they set up their own studio.

The result is a classical beauty with muted theatrical elements that come out in the colours used, providing the ideal setting for their designs. It is as if the lighting sculptures come to life in the still interior, where the colours of the various rooms feel warm, a little like typical English country houses. By remaining faithful to the atmosphere and style of the building, what emerged was a modern-chic but equally timeless version of the house. It was originally built for an attorney-general, and was now ready for a new generation.

A major additional advantage of the former music school was that a performance hall and foyer had been built behind the house in the fifties. They provided plenty of space for a studio! It was the perfect place to focus undisturbed on developing their designs. The first assistant, whom they had rather tentatively engaged, was soon joined by two more. This was also the period when the handmade lighting sculptures were taking precedence, in addition to the gallery they had set up to show their work after graduating, and the architectural and design projects they had so far been engaging in.

In the meantime, the welding shop for the sculptures has been moved to the workshop at the present head office in Naarden. The whole house is once again available to the family, which has now gained a second son. But William still has his drawing office in the attic. William: 'I do most of my work at the office, but when I am in the creative phase, I need peace and quiet. And then I work at home.' His workroom is light, with skylights built into the roof. The built-in cupboards and the ceilings have been restored with handsome panelled sections. Annet has her own separate studio at the house. In the former foyer of the school she has a large, well-lit room with windows looking out onto the garden all around. She can enjoy this view, to the accompaniment of birdsong, while working on her creations in perfect peace. The workshop where all the objects were previously made has now been converted into an austere white room that is also used as a photographic studio. It is here, with Annet as art director, that new designs are photographed and photo-shoots are done for the brochure and other purposes.

William and Annet are actually minimalists and have very few bits and pieces in their home. They derive great pleasure from the wooden staircase with its turned and milled parts, now thoroughly restored, and the iron fencing specially forged by hand.

In the bathroom too, respect for tradition is successfully combined with modern and practical domestic comfort. They wanted to retain the atmosphere of the old terrazzo floor, but they did install floor heating. Highly practical open cupboards were devised and they designed the upright washstands themselves.

The kitchen is the heart of the house. It is where they spend a lot of time and looks as if it were taken from a painting by Vermeer. It is laid with large tiles in marble and Belgian bluestone. The old basic tiles were already in the house and were moved and relaid without grouting.

In addition to the lighting sculptures and other designs of their own, such as the sofa in the living room and the glasswork collection Annet made on commission to Royal Leerdam, several 'sculptures from nature' are displayed in the house. Their love and respect for nature enables them to see the skeletons as still-lifes. Nature inspires them so much more than any other object or design. The house has an atmosphere of bygone days yet at the same time feels very much like a house of its time. As far as decoration is concerned, the rooms have been kept very frugal. 'The reflections of light on a wall and the play of shadows that go with it are so beautiful, so pure, that we can't get enough of them. It would be a shame to divert the attention from the play of light by adding all sorts of oddments and accessories.' These are clearly the words of two artists with a fascination for light. It comes as no real surprise that their artistic course, although not planned in advance, should ultimately involve lighting sculpture.

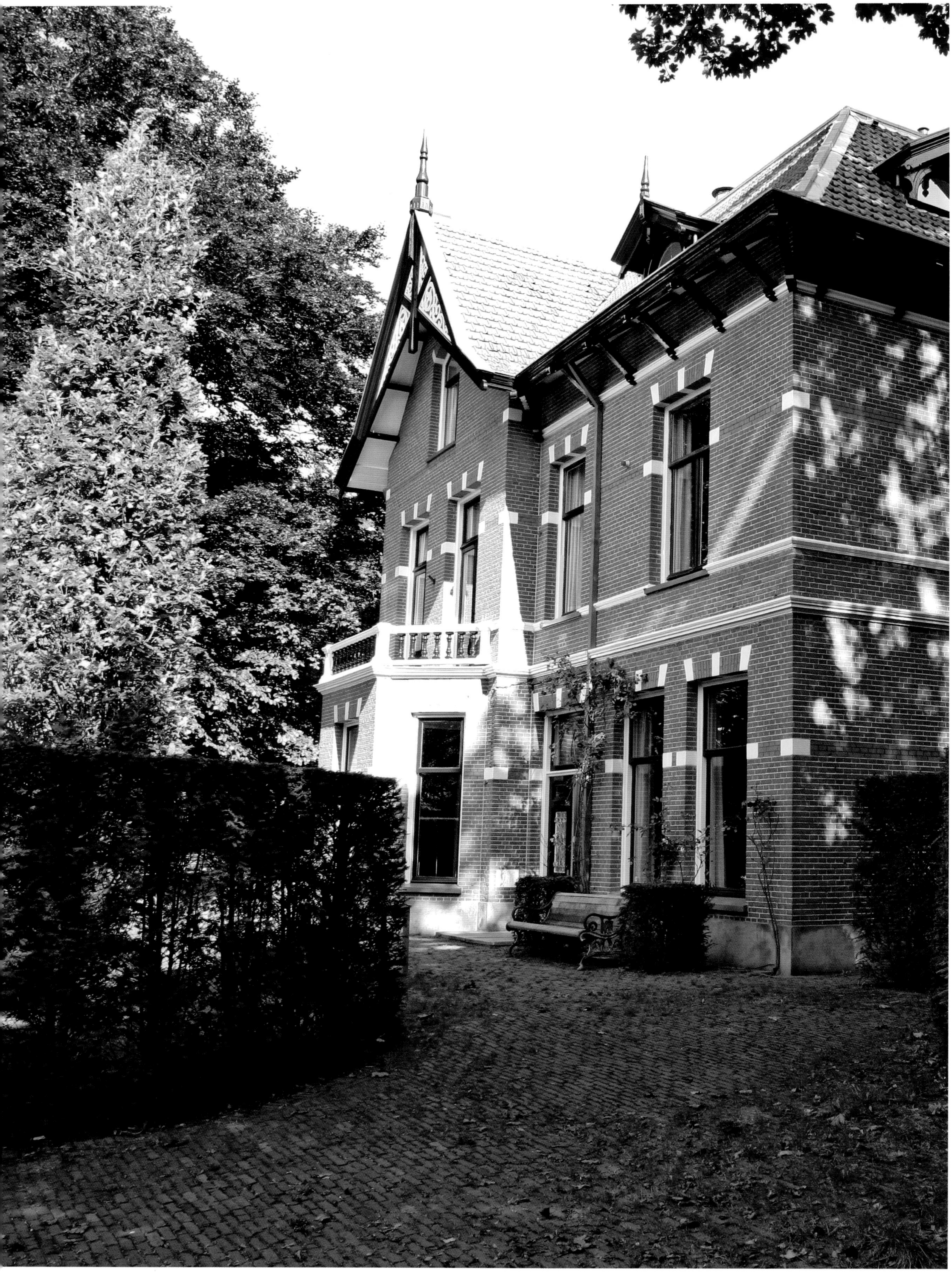

Annet and William's house, Bussum 2008

Hall at the house in Bussum, Floating Candles chandelier and wall lamps

Living room with Flower Power seat objects and a sofa designed
by William and Annet, Broom standard lamps

Living room at Bussum. Love you Love you not conical chandelier in nickel

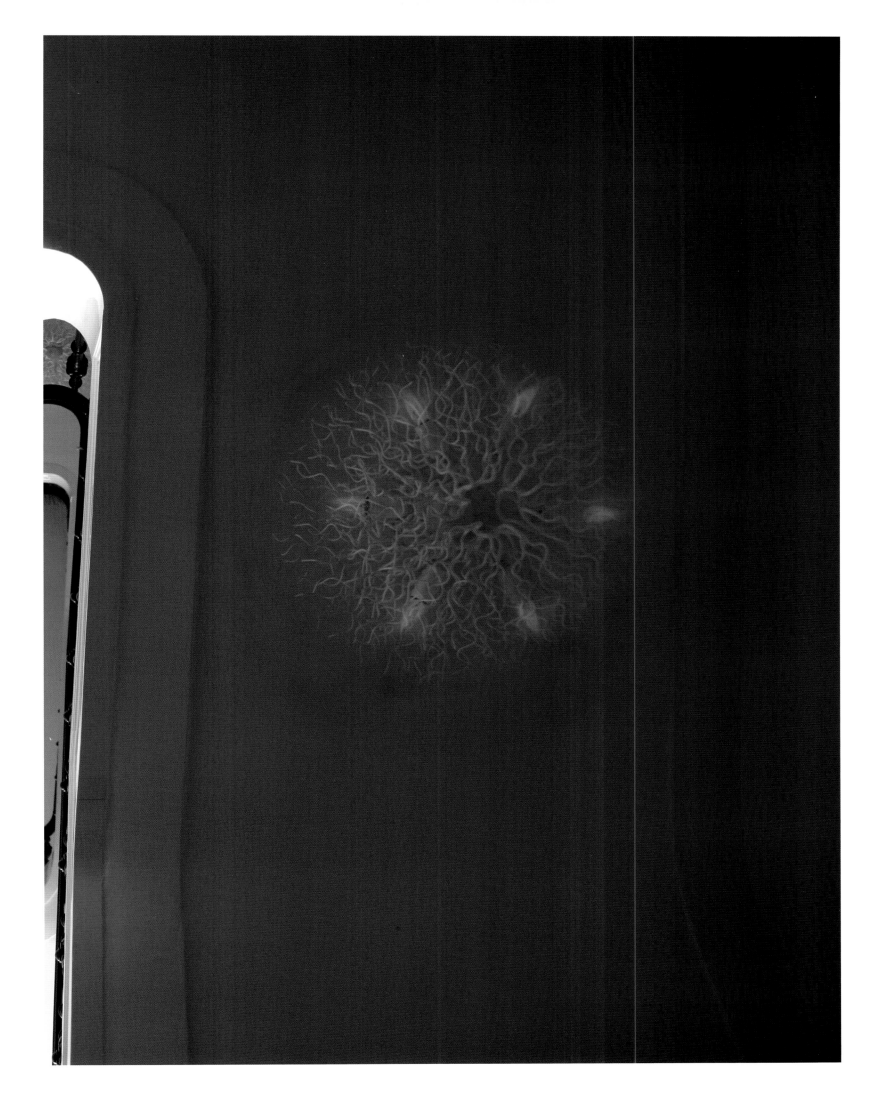

Bathroom with white Hollywood chandelier and wall lamps, washstands and cabinets designed by William

FROM SCULPTURE TO LIGHTING SCULPTURE

From Sculpture to Lighting Sculpture

'Two inspired artists going their own way

It started with the fascination for the spatial object'

—

For Annet and William, their time at art college (College of Arts, Utrecht, 1984-89) was the ideal basis for their experimentation. Annet started studying fashion but soon discovered that she had a greater affinity for sculpting and autonomous spatial design. William studied small-scale architecture and furniture design. Having graduated, he worked as a freelance designer for several Dutch designers including Rob Eckhardt (Eckhardt & Leeuwenstein), the Jan des Bouvrie studio and Premsela & Vonk.

Annet and William were often at work together in the evening in the workshop at the art college in Utrecht. They then bought their first welding equipment. After numerous sketches of various rhythms their first sculptures took shape, as well as a shared style of their own. Initially they soldered a lot and made objects in plaster, but this did not offer the transparency they were looking for. They made delicate iron objects with plate glass that caught reflections and made light an essential part of the object. They worked with such down-to-earth materials as wood, iron, zinc, glass and cement. In this period, all the objects were conceived and made on the floor.

In 1988 a naked light source was used inside the object and the sculpture was raised up to the ceiling. This is how their first lighting sculpture – *Chandelier* – was born. *Chandelier* was a great success from the very start. At that point, however, they thought it was just a one-off project. They still had not the slightest inkling of their future as designers of an independent lighting design label.

After art college, Annet exhibited her sketches and sculptures in various galleries and at exhibitions, and received a starter's grant. William received the prize for the Best Furniture Design in 1990. Light and sculpture continued to inspire both of them. Commissions from enthusiastic entrepreneurs enabled them to continue both with the development of artistic work and experimentation.

Their style is clearly recognisable in the sculptures and sketches and it also reappears in their lighting sculptures. In 1992 they made a glass object in the Amstel Park, one in which nature played a part: a glass blanket (a sort of glass patchwork) was hung up like a cloth. A work called *Tender Blue*, from the same period, which was purchased by the Architecture Institute in Rotterdam, suggests the rhythm of a Dutch landscape. The crates of stacked glass evoke the illuminated greenhouses the Netherlands are so celebrated for.

The *Mikado* staircase is an object made for a building by Piet Boon. The staircase is designed so that the object can be seen from the outside too. It is the pivotal point of the building and literally and figuratively links together the various parts of the building. A sculpture is here transformed into usable aesthetic object.

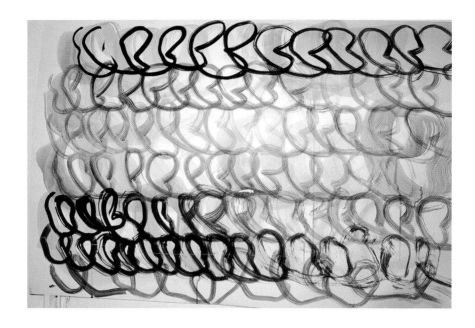

It was for a property developer who started up after the fall of the Berlin Wall that they designed the table object called *Pick Up the Pieces*. They made a symbolic table that might serve as a start for new and delicate negotiations between East and West. The tabletop was smashed with a single blow in the workshop, and then all the pieces of glass were carefully collected and polished. They looked for distinctively shaped branches in the Noordwijk woods to add to the object. They then had pipe couplings screwed onto the pieces of glass so that they could be fixed to the iron frame in such a way as to form a smooth and usable top again.

During this period, their free sculptural work carried on but the commissions also kept on pouring in. To *Chandelier* was added a collection of conical crowns and wall lamps. The new monumental chandeliers were used to adorn the University of Amsterdam. They created the nipped edges of the strips of glass using pincers they made themselves. The large lighting sculptures for the university led to *Behind The Frosted Glass*.

Annet could be found welding in the workshop every day. These were years of continuous hard work. After the frame for a lighting sculpture had been welded and all the pieces of glass had been drilled and polished, she delivered the lamps herself. In addition to the welding work, William also worked on a variety of other commissions, such as for Soap Studio, for whom he designed stands. In 1992 he designed a complete shop interior for Oogappel Opticians in Amsterdam. He and Annet also made the tables and chairs together. By working through the night, everything was perfectly on time for the opening.

Inspiration and design has always been a stage to which they have devoted a great deal of time before a new model appears. This is certainly true for the collection of poetically shaped and sand-blasted mirrors that were shown as objects in Amsterdam at the Frozen Fountain gallery in 1993.

The production process has developed step by step over the last 20 years. Whereas in the beginning William and Annet made all the objects with their own hands, in 1996 they cautiously employed and trained their first assistants. At the same time, the lighting sculptures were being made in several workshops of their own by people whom William had specially trained. The rough, sculptural, handmade character remained in every object, however. Their own style remained a key element.

Over the years, Annet and William have increasingly become 'fashion designers'. They launch their new '*haute couture* pieces' in Milan. It requires a massive amount of work to get the prototypes, the photography and everything else ready for the launch. These latest models are then finally shown to the world on austere white and/or black stands.

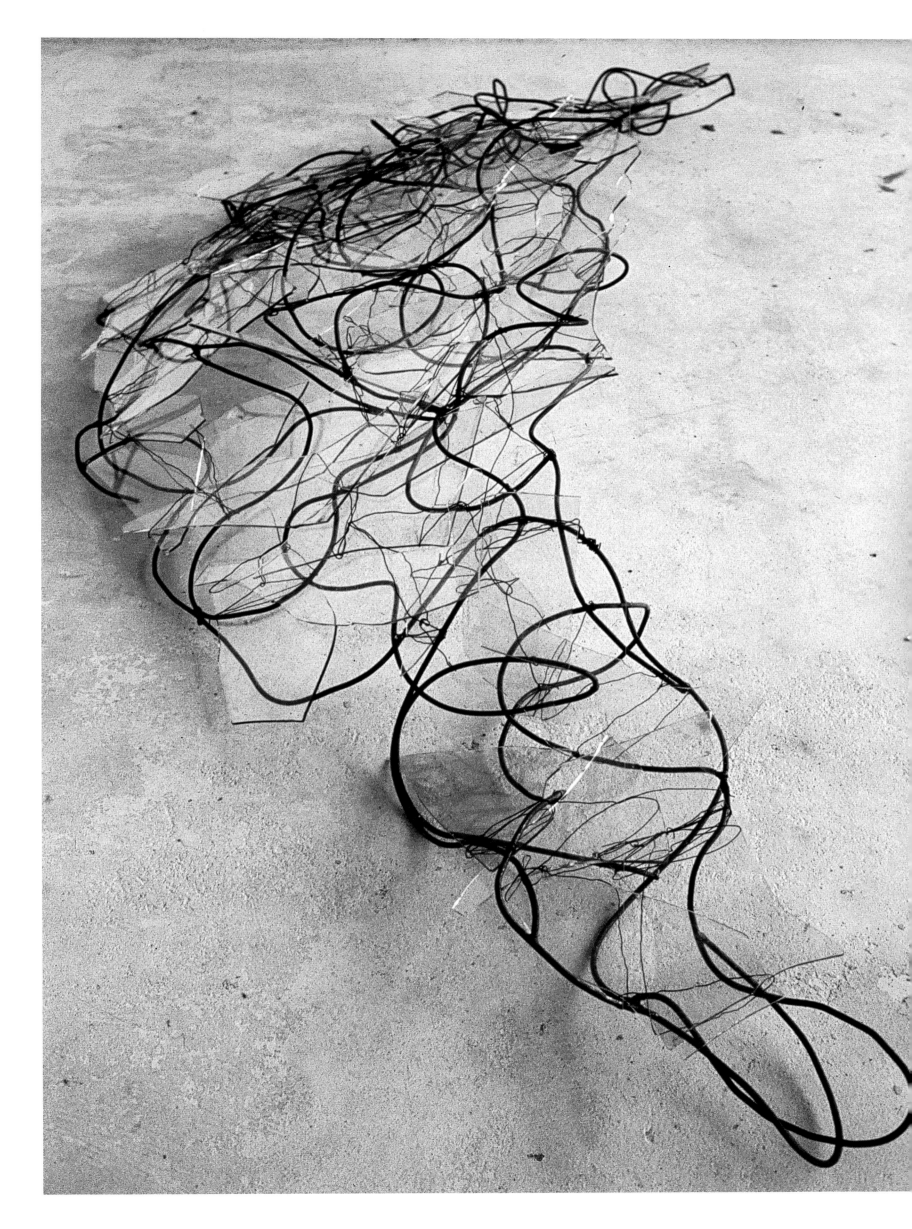

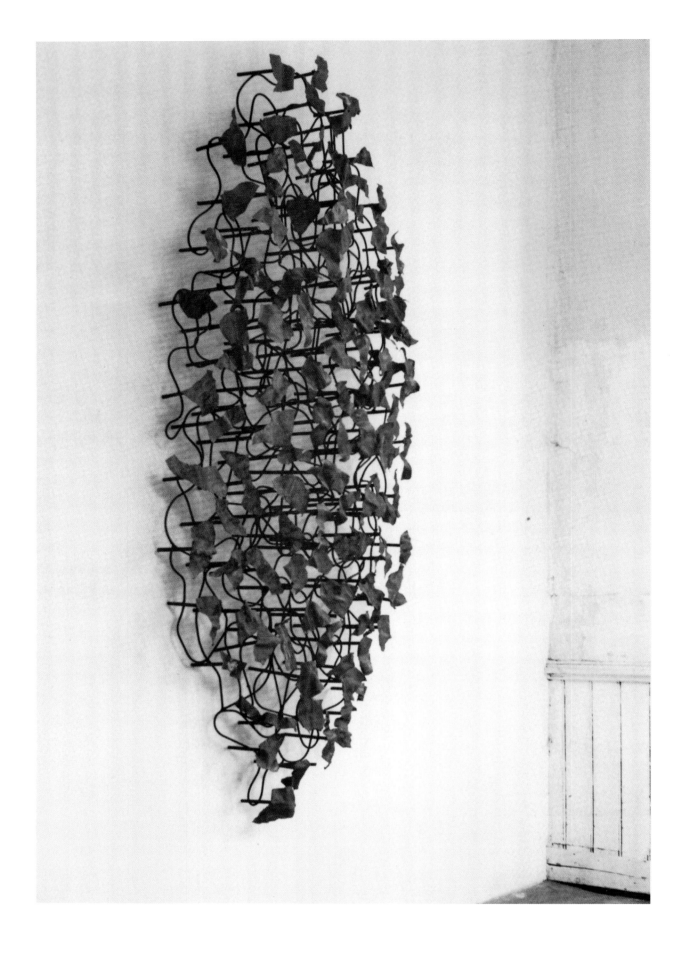

The Tender Blue, stack of Dutch crates with glass, property
of Nederlands Architectuur Instituut, Rotterdam 1990

Annet working on Chandelier, 1990

Nature mirror, Frozen Fountain exhibition, 1992

60

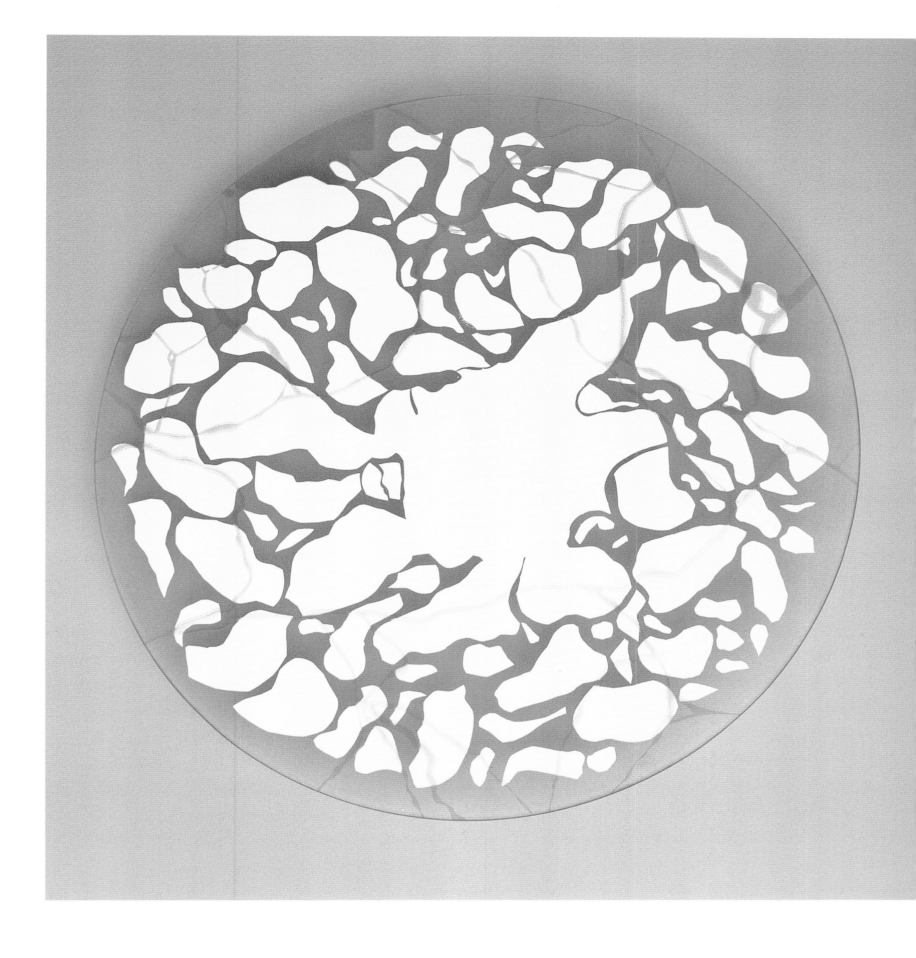

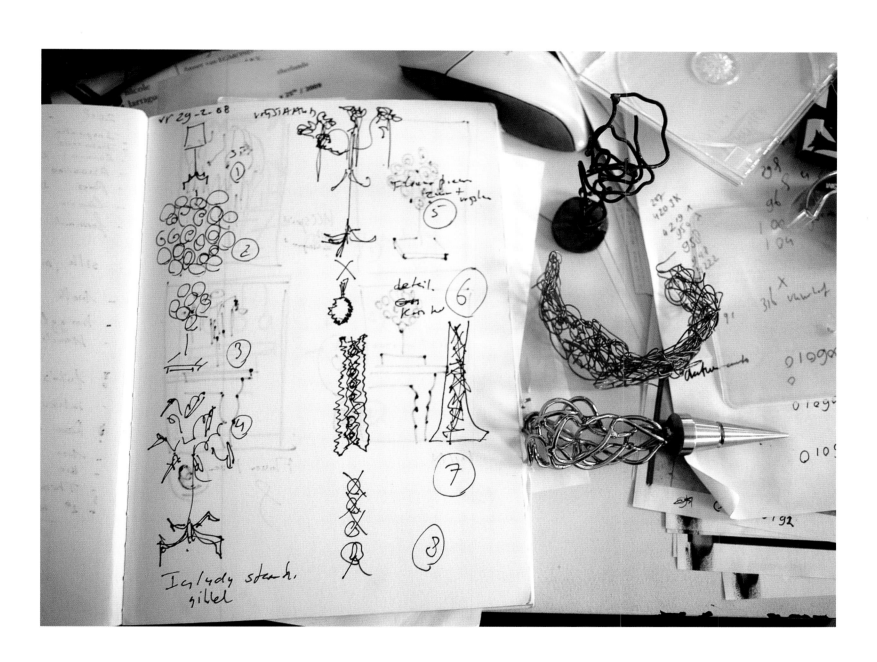

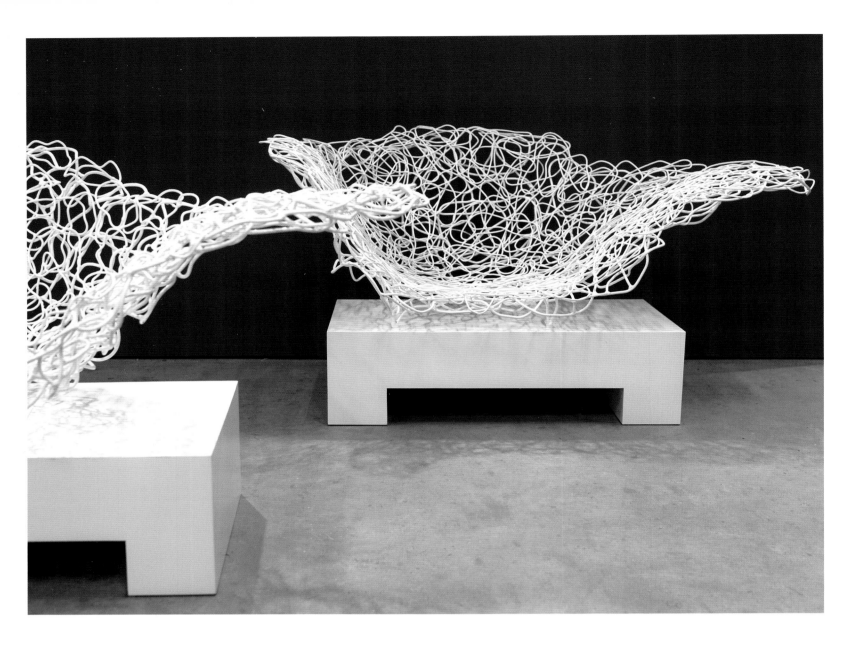

Lola prototypes on forklift truck, Naarden 2007

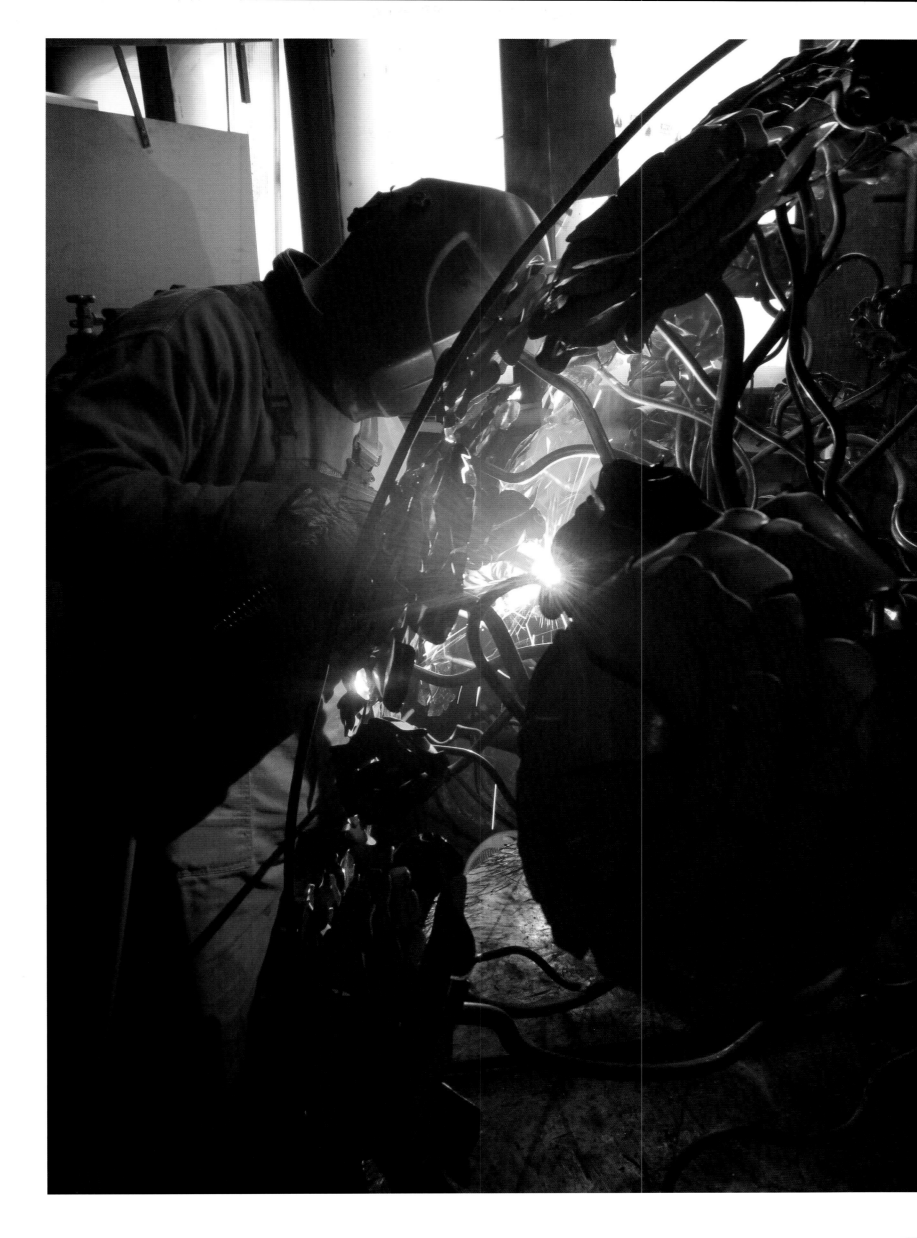

Architecture Projects

'The Sense of Order' – Gombrich

—

'Architecture is one of my greatest passions,' says William Brand. 'It's all about the experience of walking through a building ... It should be harmonious and intimate. And also, projects like that are carried out with a large group of people. That is the essential difference from product design. Designing a product is more manageable.'

William first came into contact with architecture while at art college. He worked on new interiors with Rob Eckhardt and the film-maker Wil van der Vlugt. In the late eighties the number of lifestyle advertising films increased. Advertising agencies were set up and new film studios built. The era of real interiors and interior products in advertising films dawned. Jurriaan Eindhoven was one of those who wanted a new film studio at the time. The brief went to Eckhardt & Leeuwenstein. William was given the unique opportunity of working on the job. At the same time he was a freelance designer for Jan des Bouvrie and Piet Boon.

His first major interior brief was for the Oogappel opticians in Amsterdam in 1992, a shop where the designer spectacles had to be well highlighted. The principle that William shared with the client Pieter Smit was that it had to be a professional institute but should not look too clinical. Sand-blasted glass panels were devised against which the glasses play a rhythmic game with each other. Tables and leather chairs were also specially designed and made. The chandelier and mirrors with sand-blasted designs gave the interior a style entirely its own. Even now, 17 years on, the shop still looks good.

Although Brand van Egmond's lighting sculptures are mostly decorative, William's architectural projects are above all representative of a restrained sobriety. He tries to keep every detail simple. His great example is John Pawson, the minimalist architect. William sees it all as a matter of refinement. Which is why he works out his designs down to the smallest details and designs tables, chairs and cupboards specially for each interior. William: 'The basic idea has to be carried through into the details. It is the sum of all the details that gives the overall impression. I never do anything without reason, and there is never a cupboard or wall that has not been carefully considered.' One of the elements of his philosophy is that an interior should be able to last at least fifteen years and to endure all sorts of changes. 'An interior is alive and has a soul. Whether it's an existing building or a new one, you start with the sketch. The challenge is always to solve all the technical and constructional impediments in an aesthetic way.' It is no coincidence that many of his interior designs are commissioned by companies in the fashion world. These projects have a certain panache, just like the clients. Also, clothing and jewels are shown at their best in a tranquil and well-lit interior, which is something William is very good at.

Twill, 1998
In the case of the Twill showroom that William designed, where several of the leading brands in the fashion world are shown, the request was to participate in thinking about the concept. The owner, Ruud Uijttewaal, asked whether it was possible to design the showroom for the launch of new brands so that it remained flexible. This would

make it possible to avoid a brand being permanently attached to a particular space if it was not successful. William installed a large glass partition with on one side a big showroom that can be divided up as necessary using mobile panels, and on the other two immense 'tents' that also contain presentation spaces. Cement was deliberately chosen for the floor so the effect is not too dressy. The monumental staircase leads to separate rooms where the collections of the leading brands are shown. This upward movement was a conscious choice on William's part: 'The way there is very important. When you are at the bottom of the stairs, you should get the feeling that you are now going to see something very special. This excitement has to be intensified.'

Didato, 1997

When the men's fashion shop Didato had the opportunity to double its floor area in P.C. Hooftstraat in Amsterdam, they called in William to design the shop so that it would become a business with international allure that would not be out of place in London, Milan or New York. The owners, Bert Prakke and Sjef Boersma, sell superb design collections. It was no simple task. The basement has very low ceilings and the building has a structural beam through the middle of the shop. He used the space between the beams at the bottom of the building by housing a sewing workshop and the toilets there. The arrangement is plain and clear, the materials are consistent and restfulness and space predominate once again. Everything is very light, partly due to the use of the latest indirect lighting techniques. At the back of the shop there are handmade glass changing cubicles lit from below. Here too, all the furniture was designed and made by Brand van Egmond.

Brand van Egmond head office, 2002

The leading players in the Brand van Egmond head office are light, austerity and emotion. This aesthetic industrial building in Naarden is striking for its sober, rigid, glazed facade and black frame. Once inside, you can sense the intimacy. The skylights let in the subtle play of ever-changing Dutch light. The plainly plastered walls are painted dark grey, which gives the space the feel of a warm blanket. The high ceilings give the building the atmosphere of a museum that does full justice to the large lighting sculptures. The linear interplay of the structural supporting beams in the workshop creates a graphic effect. Nothing has been left to chance. This building too has a plain cement floor with long, simple wooden tables. The handrail of the wooden staircase is integrated into the plasterwork. Big lighting objects can be viewed at eye level on the high catwalk. The eleven-metre-long transparent black curtain gives the building a homely feel.

This building was originally designed as a showroom and workshop, but the tremendous growth of the company means it now also houses the offices. The small prototypes are still conceived and made in the workshop. This is done in the quiet of the evening, when everyone has gone home.

William is currently engaged in designing a new production building for Brand van Egmond. A new challenge he takes up with great pleasure. Because although the lighting sculptures of the Brand van Egmond design label take up much of his time and are his true love, his roots are clear to see. Architecture will always be one of his passions.

Green Flower Power chandelier with Flower Power
seat objects, Brand van Egmond showroom

Broom wall lamp in toilet with concrete slab and sand-blasted glass door

Two Rhapsodys in Brand van Egmond canteen, table designed by William

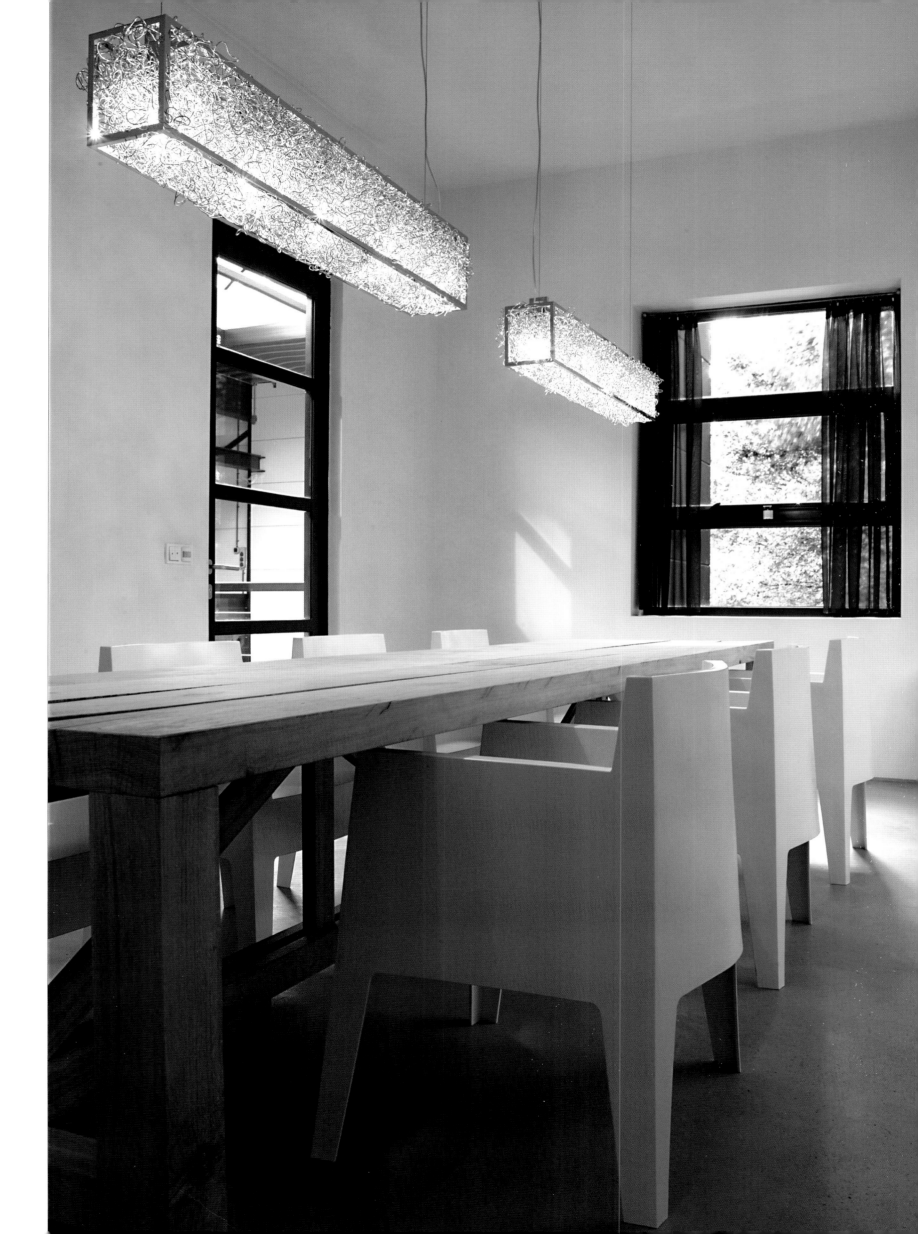

Crystal Waters domed chandelier in Brand van Egmond showroom   94

Twill showroom, Armani importer, interior design by William,
Night Watch chandelier in white, Amsterdam 1998

Twill showroom, Amsterdam 1998   96

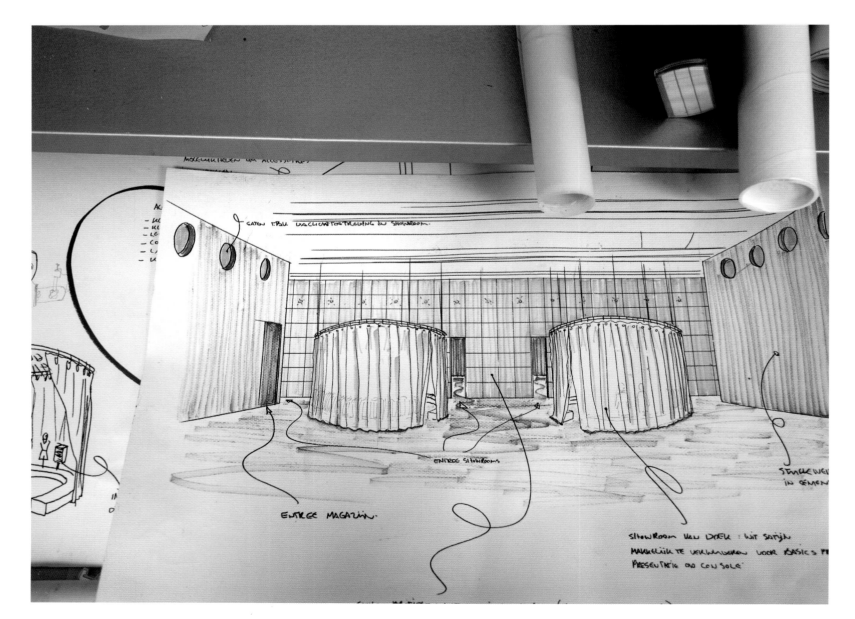

Working with other Creatives

Since William's architecture projects, more and more creative people have crossed their path. Inventive initiative-takers who are eager to discuss their plans with them. The existing collection often forms the starting point. In this way, variations on a theme like *Flower Power* result in large special editions in different shapes, colours or sizes. Clients arrive who might have a problem with their stairwell, for example, for which there are no ready-made solutions. Annet and William regard just these sorts of difficulties as a challenge. And even if a project doesn't lead to immediate execution, it can provide inspiration for a new collection.

For example, the Okura Hotel in Amsterdam had a problem with the lighting for its top floor. Annet and William were asked to help think about a solution. The problem was actually quite trivial, involving the size of the door through which the chandelier had to be brought in. This was only 90 centimetres wide, whilst the ceiling on which the lighting would have to hang was extremely high and therefore needed a generously sized lamp. This problem eventually inspired William and Annet to design *Floating Candles*, which, with no restriction of length or diameter, could be constructed on the spot.

Jamie Oliver's Fifteen restaurant, Amsterdam 2004
An unusual project for the Fifteen restaurant led to a new first: the seating objects *Sculpture on a Socle* or *S.O.S.* These seating objects have a pedestal and a sculpture. The sculpture is almost draped over the pedestal like an ornament. The seat sculptures are made of foam, with a back of nickel-plated metal that is extremely comfortable. The client chose *Crystal Waters* as a lighting object for the building.

Stadeshuys, Stavoren 2005
A lighting sculpture was ordered for the Zuiderzee suite of this 1879 town hall. This suite is a unique space where you can look though binoculars at a view of the former Zuiderzee. Next to an old painting of Prince William I it was decided to hang two *Hollywood* ceiling lights, which complemented their historical surroundings extremely well.

Hanze Gentleman's Club, Groningen 2006
On entering the Hanze Gentleman's Club you can still sense the old club atmosphere. You don't need much imagination to conjure up a picture of cigar-smoking gentlemen in leather club armchairs. The choice of the *Flower Power* chandelier was made together with an architectural firm from Groningen: black chandeliers for the club rooms themselves and made-to-measure red chandeliers for the reception area.

Neuhaus chocolaterie, Brussels 2006
The architects Desgrippes & Gobe, who designed the interiors for the branches of Neuhaus chocolaterie, chose the *Candles & Spirits* chandelier for the shops. The architects succeeded in designing a minimalist yet warm interior where the chandeliers fitted seamlessly into the luxurious environment. The handmade chocolate is respectfully presented by white-gloved assistants. 'It's fantastic to happen upon our chandelier in their chocolate shop in Tokyo,' says Annet.

Belle et Fou theatre, Berlin 2006
'We were invited to Berlin to supply lighting sculptures to the Belle et Fou theatre. Having seen the theatre, we decided, together with architecture bureau Meuser, to go for the red *Flower Power* chandeliers.' This theatrical lamp fits perfectly in this historic building, through whose corridors

Marlène Dietrich once strode. Above the bar hang specials from the same collection. It's also worth mentioning that a while ago Karl Lagerfield photographed some models in this boudoir-like setting, with *Flower Power* in the background.

Gooilust country house, 's Graveland 2007
The beautiful old Gooilust country house, owned by Natuurmonumenten, is the home of the Loggere & Willpower interior design firm and fabric agency. Unique golden *Candles & Spirits* were hung in the drawing room, whose walls are clad in authentic embossed leather. In the minimalist wing with its contemporary decoration, mischievous *Lolas* illuminate the fabrics on display.

De Hooge Vuursche mansion, Baarn 2007
For the last 10 years, Annet has been working with Mirco Cuppens and Stephan van den Akker, who run monumental sites as catering venues. 'We've done a lot of projects, like the Lindenhof country house in Delft, Voorlinden in Wassenaar and the Te Werve country house in Rijswijk.' De Hooge Vuursche mansion, which dates from 1912, is set in a rural, wooded landscape. The branch-like shadows *Hollywood* now casts on the walls serve to link the interior with the surrounding woodland.

Shanghai, 2008
In 2007 Annet and William were invited to travel to Shanghai and to take a look at a building under construction where their collection was to be exhibited. In 2008 the building was finished and the Brand van Egmond collection is now proudly displayed next to that of the artist Rietveld.

Canal-side building Amsterdam, 2008
In 2008 Annet and William were given the task of designing the lighting for an old, listed canal-side building. The architect leading the renovation of the building chose the *Delphinium* chandelier for the lighting. The flowing forged floral strips hang almost naturally in the 17th-century interior. The decoratively plastered ceilings and the elegant light combine to create a seamless interweaving of past and present.

For a lighting sculpture in the stairwell the client gave them carte blanche. 'We wanted to make a sort of installation, a mobile, but one in which the light forms a subtle bond with the plasterwork and still keeps its own identity.' The inspiration came after a visit to the opera, where roses for the singers were thrown from the balconies. They drifted down like a soft, warm applause. 'A bewitching spectacle that gave us the idea of using the rose as a starting point for this project.'

Taste the Winebar, 's Gravenhage 2008
Opposite the prime minister's turret in the stately city of The Hague can be found a modern winebar. The focus here is firmly on tasting. The wine is carefully stored in safes. Swarovski offered the possibility of designing a special chandelier for the winebar using their crystals. While William was responsible for the lighting sculpture, Otazu and Eric Kuster designed the interior.

Skins Cosmetics, Laren 2008
Skins Cosmetics sells exclusive perfumes and cosmetics. For its shop in Laren, it chose Candles and Spirits, making for a beautiful interplay of contrasts in a building where the focus is on scent, quality and emotion.

Athens, Greece 2008
In 2008, together with the NTU architectural firm, Annet and William produced the large, monumental Hollywood chandeliers for a department store in Athens. Positioning the chandeliers behind one another in the high-ceilinged space creates a repetition that contributes to the feeling of grandeur.

Jamie Oliver's restaurant Fifteen, Sculpture on Socle
(S.O.S.) in the passage, Amsterdam 2004

Restaurant Fifteen, Crystal Waters domed chandelier
and S.O.S. couch, Amsterdam 2004

Nickel Candles and Spirits chandelier with black swarowsky crystals, Stavoren 2004

WORKING WITH OTHER CREATIVES

Hollywood ceiling lights with a bronze coating, Stavoren 2004

De Hooge Vuursche country house hotel, staircase with
nickel Hollywood ceiling light, Baarn 2007

These nickel Candles and Spirits hang in Neuhaus outlets all over the world, Brussels 2006

Paul Noyen shoe shop, nickel Delphinium chandelier, Amsterdam 2008

WORKING WITH OTHER CREATIVES

Villa Nova shoe shop, Lolas in stainless steel, Laren 2008

Wine bar opposite government buildings, special object
designed by William, The Hague 2008

Behind the Scenes

'In every lighting sculpture we design, we stay close to our initial feelings and those feelings are precisely what we want to bring out in the photos.'

Before a new design is shown to the world, a great deal has to happen behind the scenes. How will the lighting sculpture be presented, in what atmosphere, how does one create an iconic picture that sums up every aspect of the design, without using words? It's behind the scenes that something magical is born.

'I want to communicate lines, form, outlines and the experience. As a whole, it has to be both graphic and stylish. I sketch everything out on a blank piece of white paper, and the act of drawing gives an increasingly clear picture of the setting for the new design. You think of a picture, use the atmosphere as your starting point and move towards the concept', says Annet. Everything is planned and set up in advance down to the minutest detail. For example, it is with good reason that we look for a model among the people we know, such as Annet's friend Conny. The make-up is done by a professional, but apart from that Annet directs everything herself. She decides on the position of the camera, chooses the best shot and controls the manipulation of the image afterwards.

'In every lighting sculpture we design, we stay close to our initial feelings and those feelings are precisely what we want to bring out in the photos.' Inspiration for the photo shoots comes from sources like fashion photography and the work of the artist René Magritte. You can always detect some humour in the photos too. 'I enjoy turning a photo into a real composition. The picture must grip you immediately, without the need for words.'

For *Lola* the key words are sensuality and female independence. This is what the bandages allude to.

'A suspended candlestick conveys a strong magical and mysterious presence', believes Annet. The inspiration for the suspended candlesticks for the *Floating Candles* photoshoot came from the Harry Potter film. 'Some images are visually so strong that they get inside your mind.' Leontien, her muse, didn't have an easy time of it during the shoot. Annet wanted her body to be mirrored in all the *Floating Candles'* nickel-plated bowls, creating a sort of magical picture reminiscent of Magritte. Many hours of posing and photography eventually yielded the desired result.

The copper chandeliers that often hang in 17th-century churches were the inspiration behind *Night Watch*, a title which of course refers to Rembrandt's most famous work. The photo was also supposed to have a 17th-century feel and that's why a chequered black and white floor was chosen, like those that can be seen in many paintings from the Golden Age. 'The evening before the photoshoot we were still frantically painting black and white squares on the floor so that shooting could start straight away the following morning. From the many photos we ultimately chose the most spontaneous one, the one where our sons are holding the lamp and swinging it back and forth.'

Masked ball, private party given by Annet, inspired by the film Eyes Wide Shut, 2009

Coco chandelier in nickel with glass crystals, 2009

BEHIND THE SCENES

SOLDER

3

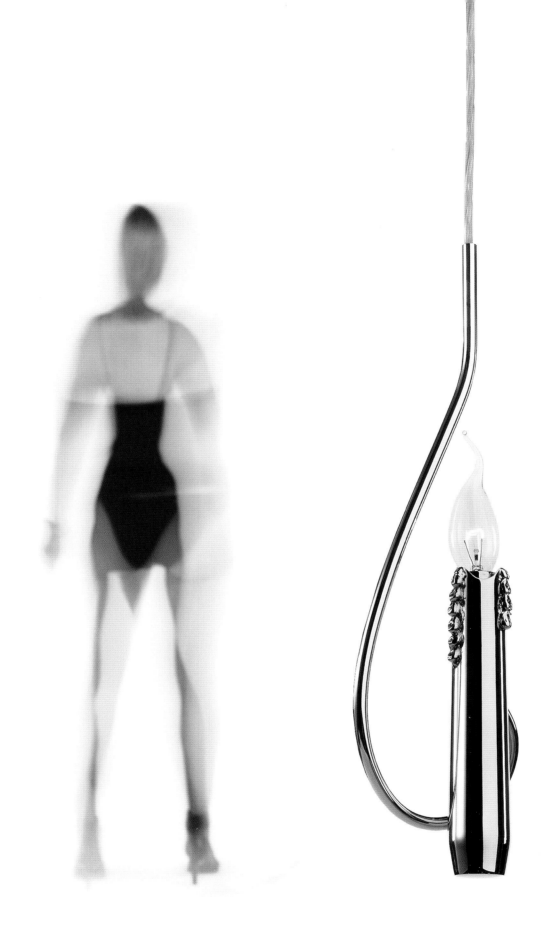

Planet Earth – Going Global

Brand van Egmond have now expanded their sphere of work to include the whole world. And not only as far as inspiration is concerned: their lighting sculptures have found their way to places all over the planet. Annet and William greatly enjoy the trips they have to make for this purpose. 'It is wonderful to be part of the earth, to go to places that are quite inaccessible or else extremely hectic. It gives us energy and inspiration.' They will not easily forget the first time they saw their name in Chinese displayed on a wall in Shanghai in 2008. It was like the ultimate affirmation of their ambition to express a universal language in their lighting sculptures. The scene showing Prince Willem-Alexander and Princess Maxima beneath their chandeliers at the World Expo in Zaragoza in 2008 was of course also memorable. But each presentation in Milan, Kortrijk and other European venues is always exciting and special.

From Tokyo to Milan, from New York to Kortrijk, from Zaragoza to Frankfurt and from Shanghai to Cologne, Brand van Egmond lighting sculptures effortlessly play their part as true global citizens, in the guise of the seductive *Lola*, the mysterious *Floating Candle* or *Broom* the diligent worker.

Black Flower Power chandeliers, window display at
Marlies Dekkers boutique, Rotterdam 2006

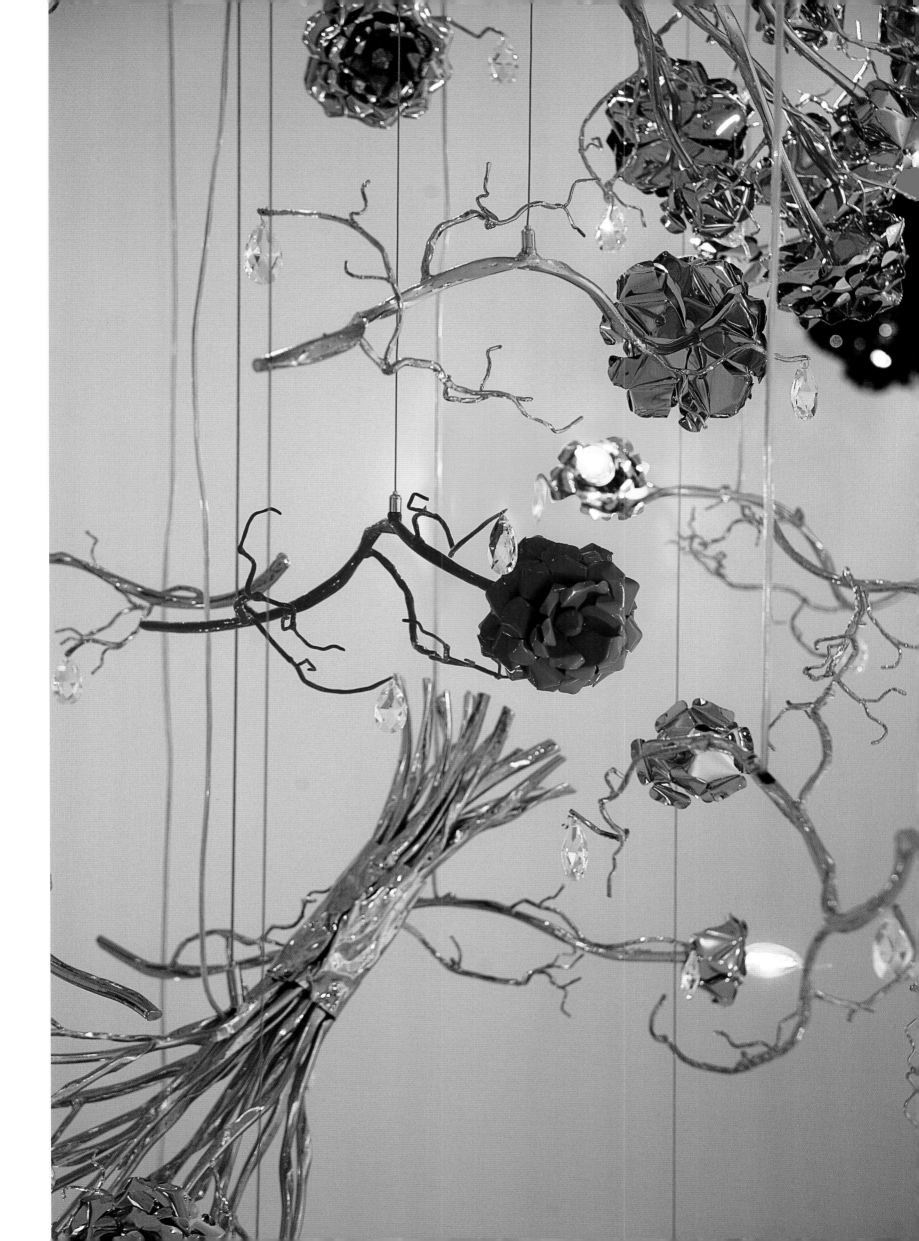

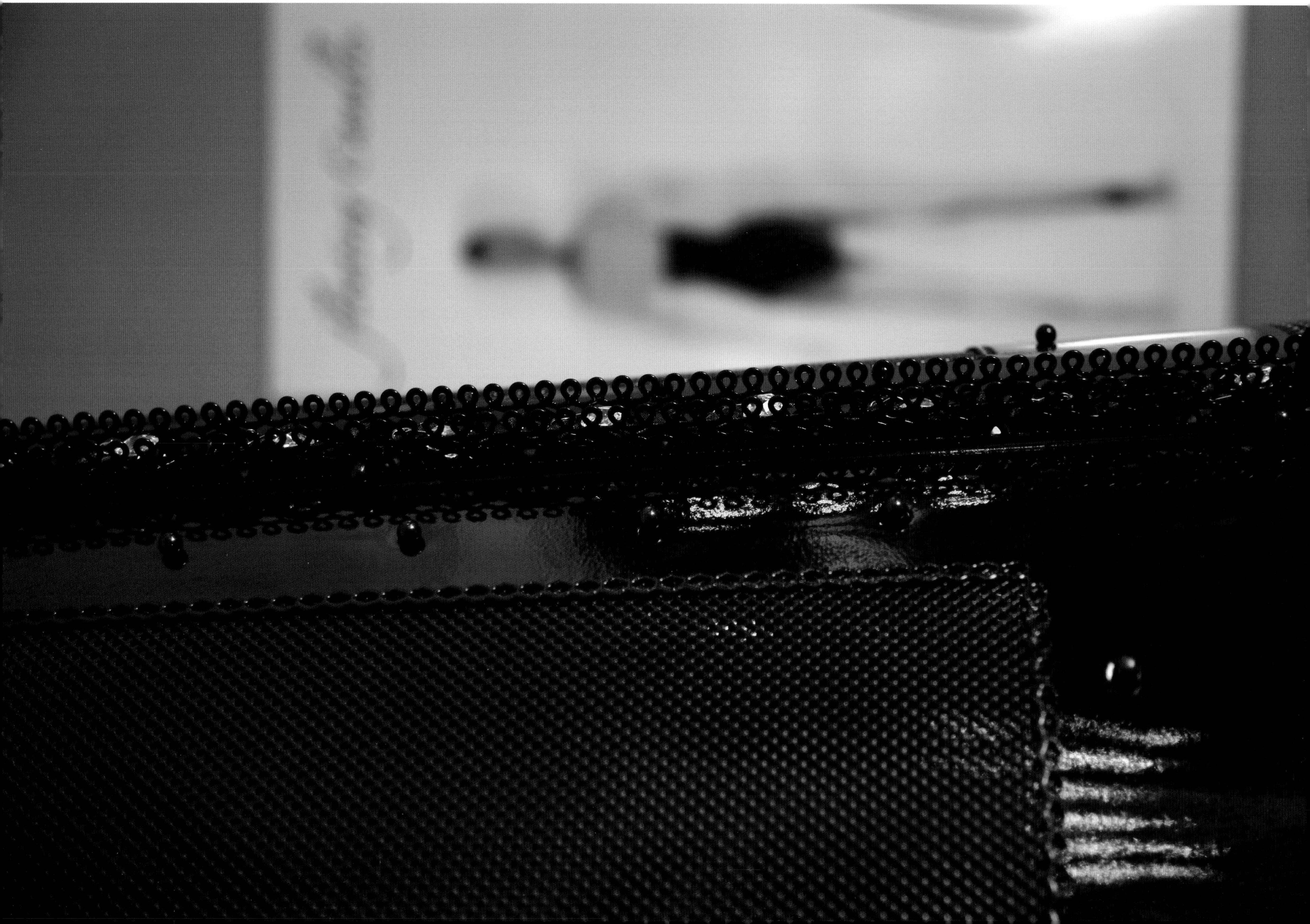

Collection
— Inspiration

'What inspires us is nature, Holland's light, and all the spiritual and inexplicable things we encounter on our journey.

It all starts with a longing.

We reflect in wonder on what Planet Earth has to offer.

An idea, a concept, is sometimes near at hand, sometimes further off.

We are touched by the pattern of the fire escapes in New York, a pile of African gourds, the purity of a candle's flame, raindrops in a pool of water.

The combination of movement and silence enables us to give free rein to the act of creation and to be at one with nature. The invisible, which was hidden, becomes visible.'

Chandelier

— *Repetition and Meaning*

Candles and Spirits

— *Form Rhyme Reason*

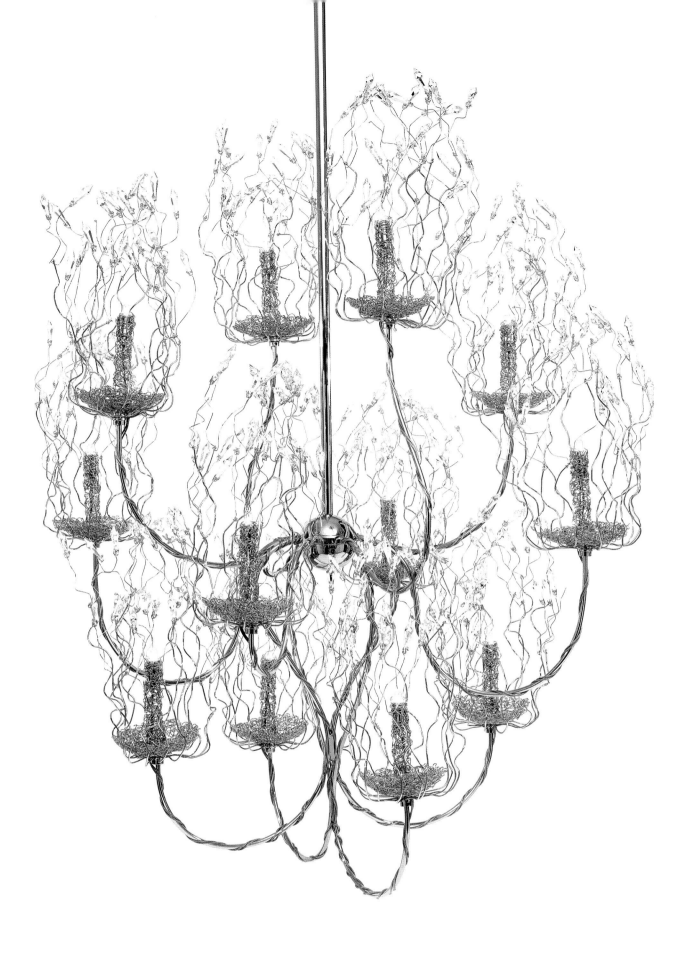

Hollywood

— *Down to
Earth going
Glamour*

Crystal Waters   — *Transparency and Shadowy Silhouettes*

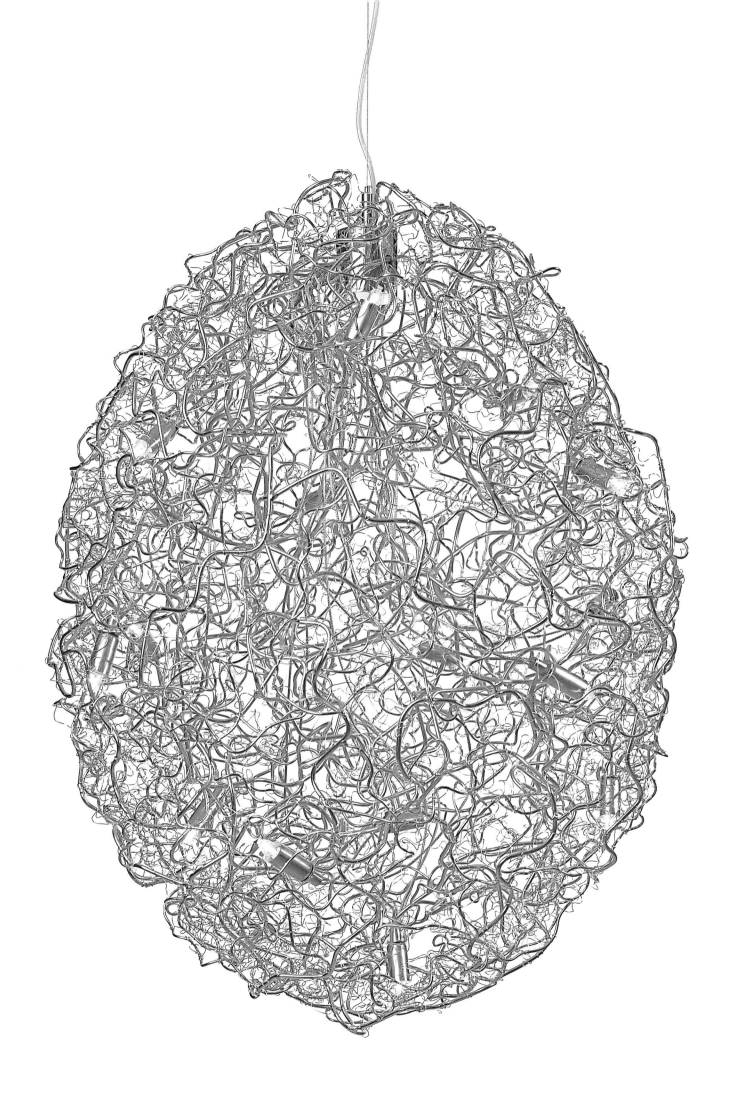

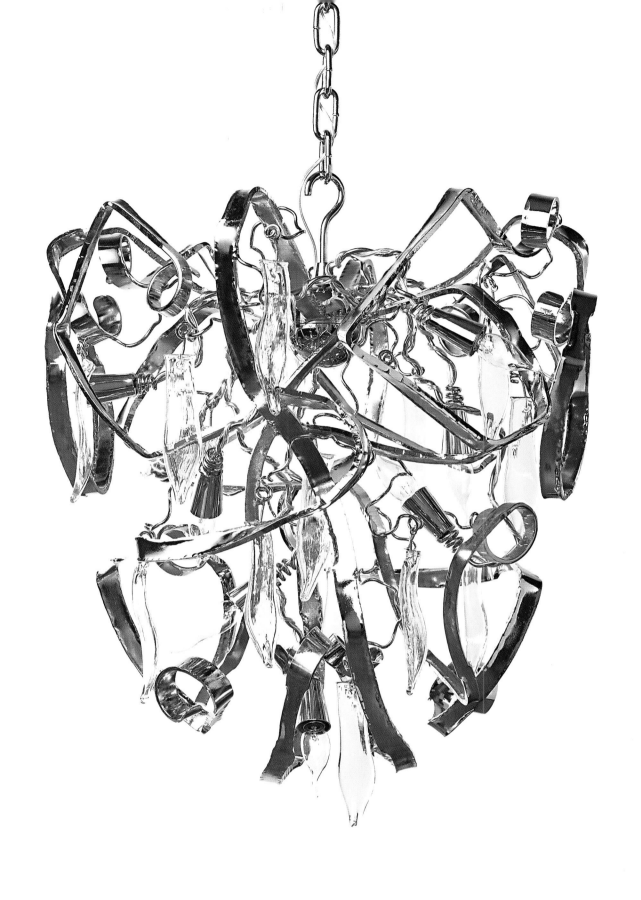

Delphinium   *— Pioneer*
of Light

Broom

— Discover Objects and Tools

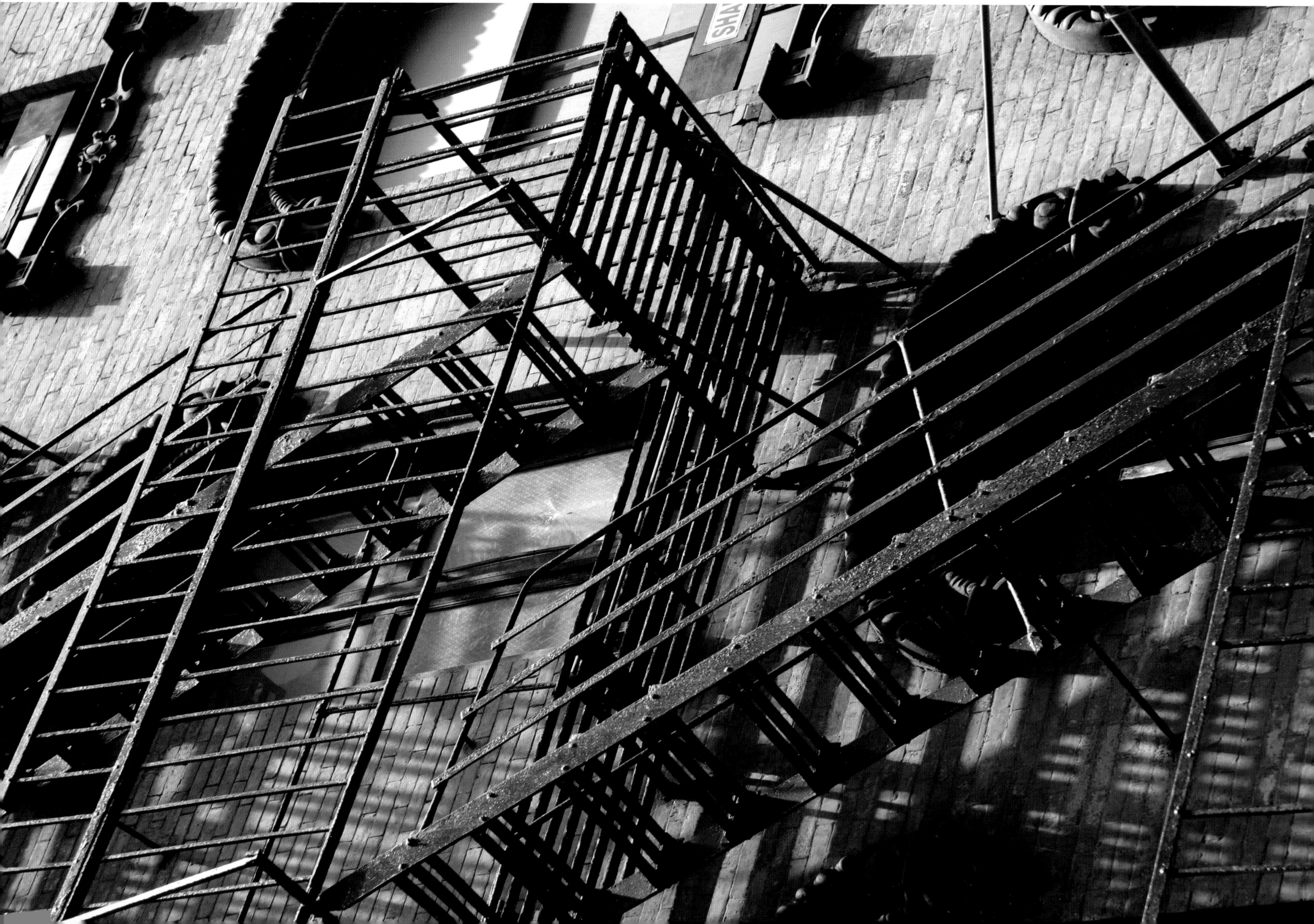

Flower Power   — *Design is Sensuality*

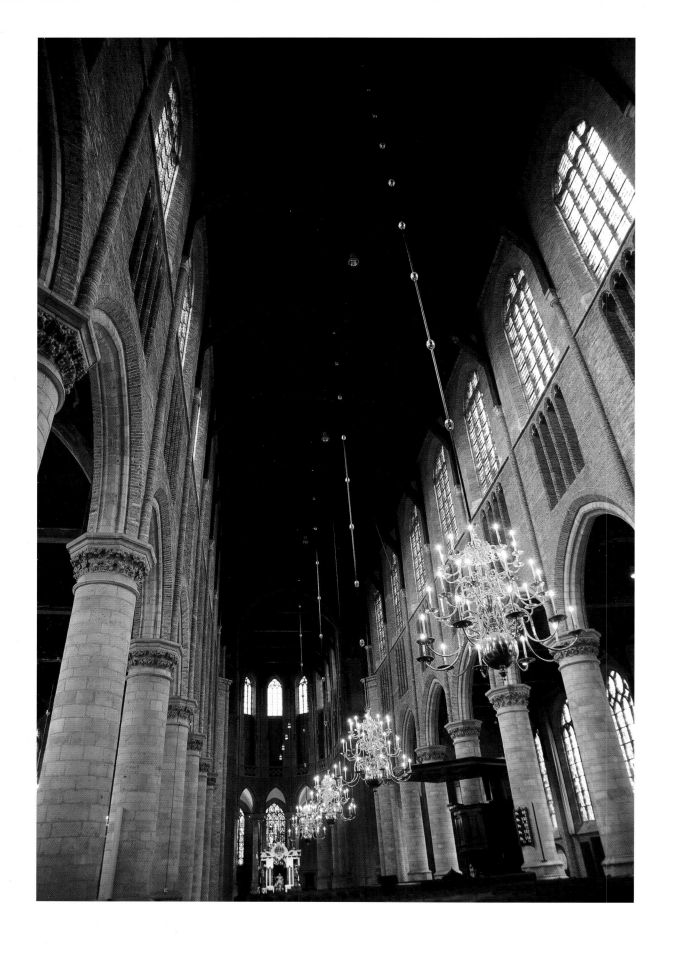

Night Watch — *Dutch Icons*

Lola — *Sensual*
Lola

Floating Candles

— *Pure Magic*

Love You
Love You Not

— *Romantic*
Love You
Love You Not ...

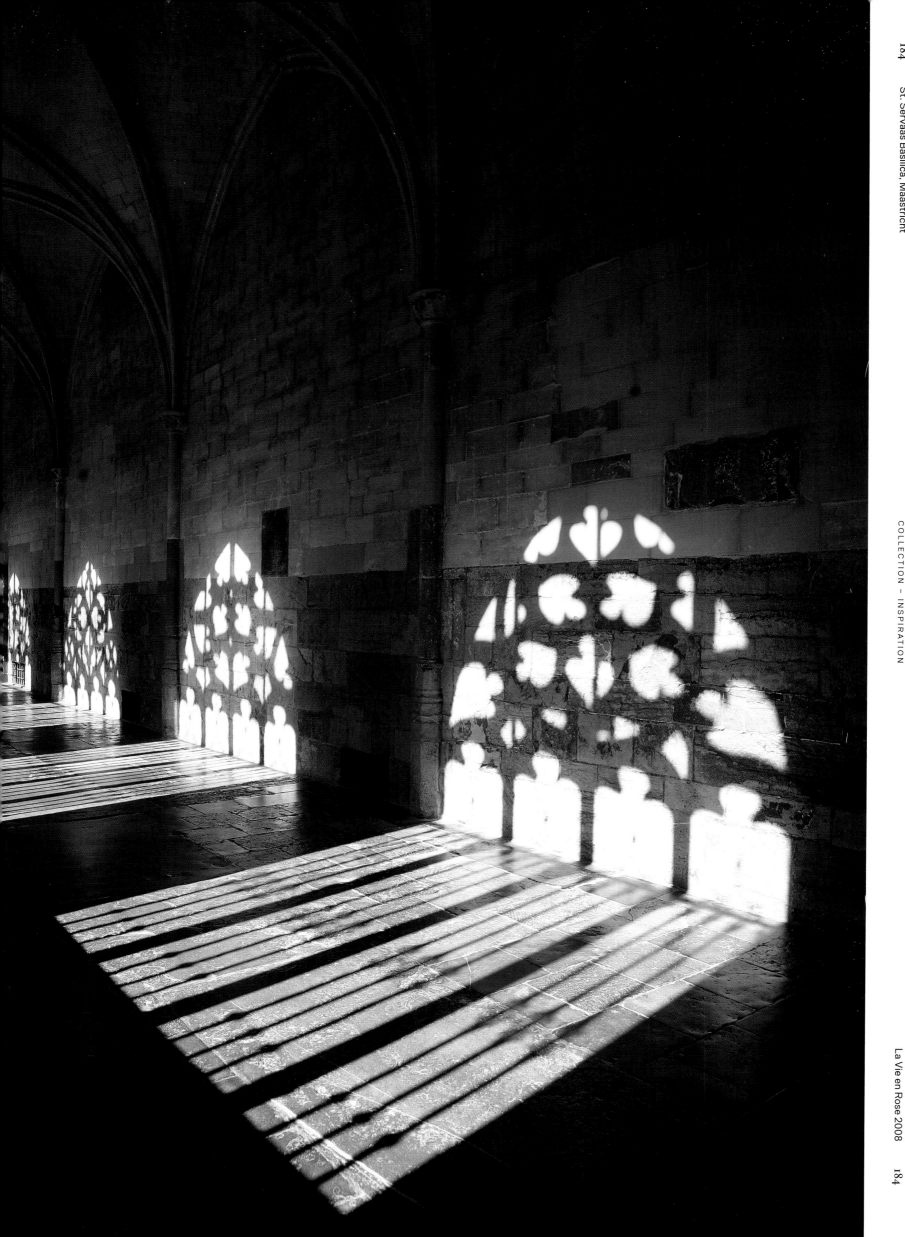

La Vie en Rose

— *Symbol of Western Spirituality*

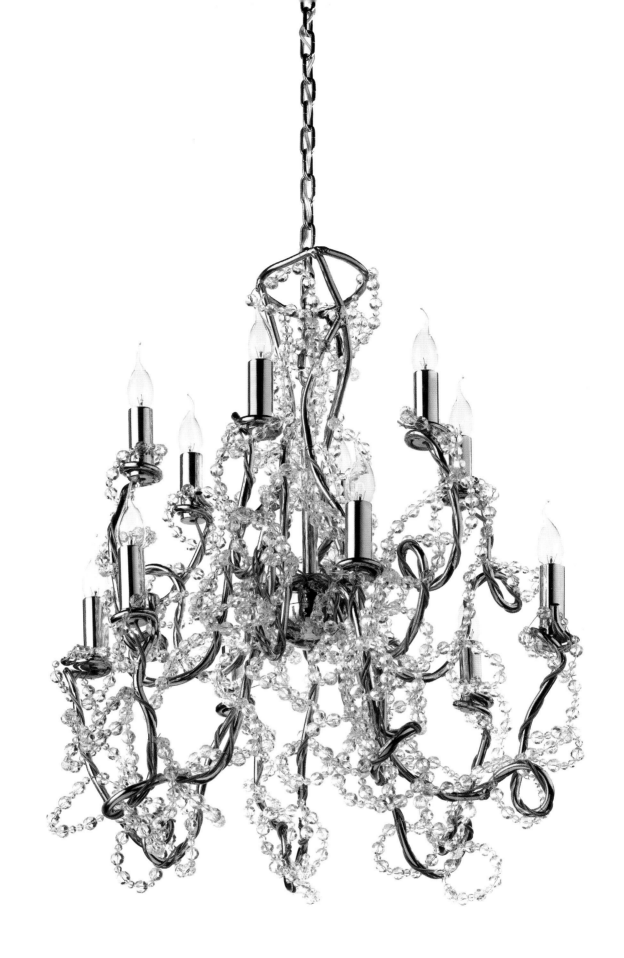

Coco   *— Fashion meets*
Design

Icy Lady — *Refined Tranquility*

Flower Power   *— Perfume Experience*

© 2009 Uitgeverij Terra Lannoo B.V.
Postbus 614, 6800 AP Arnhem
info@terralannoo.nl
www.terralannoo.nl
Uitgeverij Terra is part of the Belgian Lannoo Group

Authors
Annet van Egmond, Freija Somers and Annelies ter Brugge
Image editor
Annet van Egmond
Design
Coppens Alberts, Amsterdam
Printing and binding
Printer, Trento (Italy)

Picture credits
Alexander van Berge: p. 50, 96, 97, 99, 101
Alexander van Berge and Annet van Egmond: p. 47, 68, 92,
93, 94, 95, 100, 101, 102 103, 112, 113, 114, 115, 120, 121, 122,
123, 149, 173
Vincent Brand: p. 48
William Brand: p. 66, 69, 76, 77, 82, 83, 126, 127, 128, 178
Erik Buis: p. 2, 10
Raphaël Drent: p.30, 31
Annet van Egmond: p. 22-23, 28, 29, 32, 34, 36, 37, 38, 39,
40-41, 42, 43, 44, 45, 46, 49, 53, 59, 61, 62, 64, 65, 70, 72, 73,
74, 75, 78-79, 80, 81, 84, 87, 88-89, 90, 91, 104, 131, 138, 140,
142, 144, 146, 148, 150, 151, 153, 154, 155, 156, 158-159, 160, 162,
163, 164, 166, 168, 170, 172, 174, 176, 180, 182, 184, 186, 188,
190
Georg Fatseas: p. 132, 133
Marco Hamoen: p. 16
Marco Hamoen and Annet van Egmond: p. 24, 25, 26, 27,
35, 81, 108, 109, 110, 111, 116, 117, 118, 119, 124, 125, 128-129,
134, 136, 137, 139, 141, 143, 145, 165, 167, 169, 171, 175, 177, 179,
181, 183, 185, 187, 189, 191
Natascha Meuser en Eberhard Hoch: p. 130
Freya Somers: p. 152
Freya Somers, Annet van Egmond: p. 18
Marco Sweering: p. 58

ISBN 978-90-8989-080-1
NUR 454, 656